Preface

The book titled IGNOU BCS-040 Statistical Techniques: Previous Year Unsolved Question Papers is designed to serve as a valuable resource for students pursuing the BCS (Bachelor of Computer Science) program from the Indira Gandhi National Open University (IGNOU). The subject of Statistical Techniques (BCS-040) is a core part of the curriculum, offering essential knowledge in the field of statistics, data analysis, and probability theory-key areas that play a significant role in computing and problem-solving in various domains of science and technology.

This book contains a comprehensive collection of unsolved question papers from previous years. It has been compiled with the goal of helping students to:

Understand the pattern and structure of the questions asked in the BCS-040 exams.

Enhance problem-solving skills by practicing a wide variety of questions.

Prepare thoroughly for the examination by attempting these papers under real-time conditions.

Identify important topics and frequently asked questions for better revision and time management.

By working through these question papers, students will be able to assess their strengths and weaknesses, develop effective exam strategies, and be better prepared to face their final exams with confidence.

We hope this book proves to be a useful tool in your exam preparation journey. We wish all students the very best in their studies and future endeavors.

Table of Contents

Bachelor Of Computer Application
(Bca - Revised)
Chapter 1: Term-End Examination, June 2014
Bcs - 040: Statistical Techniques

Time: 2 Hours
Maximum Marks: 50
Note: (i) Attempt both Sections i.e. Section A and Section B.
(ii) Attempt any four questions from Section A.
(iii) Attempt any three questions from Section B.
(iv) Use of Non-scientific calculator is allowed.

Section A

1. With the help of a suitable example, describe the term "Probability Distribution". How does the Binomial Distribution differ from the Poisson Distribution? **5**

2. Suppose A and B are two independent events associated with a random experiment. If the probability of occurrence of either A or B equals 0.6, while the probability that only A occurs equals 0.4, determine the probability of occurrence of event B. **5**

3. A sample of size n=50n = 50n=50 is drawn from a population of 200 observations. If the standard deviation of the data is 22, find the standard error. **5**

4. Construct a Model ANOVA table for one-way classification. **5**

5. Write short notes on any two: **5**
(a) t-test for Mean
(b) F-test for equality of two variances
(c) Chi-square test for independence of Attributes.

Section B

6. Using the regression line $\hat{Y} = 90 + 50X$, fill up the values in the table below:

Sample No. (i)	12	21	15	1	24
x_i	0.96	1.28	1.65	1.84	2.35
y_i	138	160	178	190	210

After filling the table, compute the parameters R and R^2, and interpret the correlation between X and Y. **10**

7. What do you understand by the term forecasting? With a suitable example, discuss the relation between forecasting and future planning. Briefly discuss both forecasting models. **10**

8. Differentiate between the following (any two):
(a) Linear and circular systematic sampling
(b) Z-test and t-test
(c) Correlation and Regression **10**

9. (a) Compare and contrast Random Sampling with Non-Random Sampling. Briefly discuss the methods involved in the selection of any simple random sample. **5**

(b) Calculate an estimate of the Median for the following data:

Here's the table format you requested: **5**

Class	**0-24.9**	**25-49.9**	**50-74.9**	**75-99.9**	**100-124.9**	**125-149.9**
Frequency	6	11	14	16	13	10

Bachelor Of Computer Application
(Bca - Revised)
Chapter 2: Term-End Examination, December 2014
Bcs - 040: Statistical Techniques

Time: 2 Hours
Maximum Marks: 50
Note: (i) Attempt both Sections i.e. Section A and Section B.
(ii) Attempt any four questions from Section A.
(iii) Attempt any three questions from Section B.
(iv) Use of Non-scientific calculator is allowed.

Section A

1. Given the following sample of 20 numbers:
12, 41, 48, 58, 14, 43, 50, 59, 15, 45, 52, 72, 18, 45, 54, 78, 41, 47, 56, 79
(a) Compute mean, variance, and standard deviation.
(b) If the largest value in the above set of numbers is changed to 500,
to what extent are the mean and variance affected by the change? Justify your answer. **5**

2. The probability that at least one of the two independent events occurs is 0.5. Probability that the first event occurs but not the second is 3/25. Also, the probability that the second event occurs but not the first is 8/25. Find the probability that none of the two events occurs. **5**

3. Calls at a telephone switchboard occur at an average rate of 6 calls per 10 minutes. Suppose the operator leaves for a 5-minute coffee break. What is the probability that exactly two calls occur while the operator is away? **5**

4. A Statistics professor has given five tests. A student scored 70, 75, 65, 80, and 95 respectively in the five tests. The professor decides to determine his grade by randomly selecting a sample of 3 test scores. Construct the sampling distribution for this process. **5**

5. Briefly discuss any two of the following:
(a) Goodness of fit test
(b) Test about the mean for paired values
(c) Regression $\mathbf{2\frac{1}{2} + 2\frac{1}{2} = 5}$

Section B

6. What do you understand by the term "Time Series"? Discuss all the categories in which Time Series is classified (in 100 words each). **10**

7. Discuss the term Systematic Sampling. Differentiate between Linear and Circular systematic sampling. Give two advantages and limitations of Systematic Sampling. **10**

8. A group of 1650 school children were classified according to their performance in school tests and family economic level. Test if there is any association between these two attributes (Given $\chi^2_{0.05}(9) = 16.918$). **10**

Economic Level \ Performance	Very Good	Good	Average	Poor	Total
Very Rich	4	7	16	25	52
Rich	13	37	79	73	202
Average	105	372	298	175	950
Poor	35	213	75	123	446
Total	157	629	468	396	1650

9. A hosiery mill wants to estimate how its monthly costs are related to its monthly output rate. For that, the firm collects data regarding its costs and output for a sample of nine months as given below:

Output (Tons)	**1**	**2**	**4**	**8**	**6**	**5**	**8**	**9**	**7**
Production Cost (Thousands of dollars)	2	3	4	7	6	5	8	8	6

(a) Calculate the best linear regression line.

(b) Use this regression line to predict the firm's monthly costs if they decide to produce 4 tons per month. **10**

Bachelor Of Computer Application
(Bca - Revised)
Chapter 3: Term-End Examination, June 2015
Bcs - 040: Statistical Techniques

Time: 2 Hours
Maximum Marks: 50
Note: (i) Attempt both Sections i.e. Section A and Section B.
(ii) Attempt any four questions from Section A.
(iii) Attempt any three questions from Section B.
(iv) Use of Non-scientific calculator is allowed.

Section A

1. In order to find the correlation coefficient between two variables X and Y from 20 pairs of observations, the following calculations were made:

$$\sum x = 15, \sum y = -6, \sum xy = 50, \sum x^2 = 61, and \sum y^2 = 90.$$

Calculate the correlation coefficient and the slope of the regression line of Y on X. **5**

2. Suppose 2% of the items made in a factory are defective. Find the probability that there are:
(i) 3 defectives in a sample of 100,
(ii) no defectives in a sample of 50. **5**

3. Telephone directories have telephone numbers which are combinations of the ten digits 0 to 9. The observer notes the frequency of occurrence of these digits and wants to test whether the digits occur with the same frequency or not (α=0.05\alpha = 0.05α=0.05). The data are given below:
(Given that χ0.052(9)=16.918) **5**

Digits	0	1	2	3	4	5	6	7	8	9
Frequency	99	100	82	65	50	77	88	57	82	30

4. Fit a linear trend y = a + b $*$ Demand to the data collected in a unit manufacturing umbrellas, given in the following table: **5**

Month	1	2	3	4	5	6
Demand	46	56	54	43	57	56

5. The mean weekly sales of soap bars in different departmental stores was 146.3 bars per store. After an advertisement campaign, the mean weekly sales of 22 stores for a typical week increased to 153.7 and showed a standard deviation of 17.2. Was the advertisement campaign successful at a 5% level of significance?
(Given $t_{21}(0.05) = 2.08$) **5**

6. Write two merits and two demerits of Median. An incomplete frequency distribution is given as follows:

Class Interval (C.I.)	**10 - 20**	**20 - 30**	**30 - 40**	**40 - 50**	**50 - 60**	**60 - 70**	**70 - 80**
Frequency	12	30	?	65	?	25	18

Given that the median value of 200 observations is 46, determine the missing frequencies using the median formula. **5**

Section B

7. A chemical firm wants to determine how four catalysts differ in yield. The firm runs the experiment in three of its plants, types A, B, C. In each plant, the yield is measured with each catalyst. The yield (in quintals) is as follows: Perform an ANOVA and comment on whether the yield due to a particular catalyst is significant or not at a 5% level of significance. (Given $F_{3,6} = 4.76$) **10**

Plant	Catalyst 1	Catalyst 2	Catalyst 3
A	2	1	2
B	3	2	1
C	1	3	3

8. Find and plot the regression line of y on x on a scatter diagram for the data given below: **10**

Speed (km/hr)	30	40	50	60
Stopping Distance (feet)	160	240	330	435

9. In an air pollution study, a random sample of 200 households was selected from each of 2 communities. The respondent in each house was asked whether or not anyone in the house was bothered by air pollution. The responses are tabulated below (Given $\chi^2{}_1 0.052 = 3.841$):

Community	Yes	No	Total
I	43	157	200
II	81	119	200
Total	124	276	400

Can the researchers conclude that the two communities are bothered differently by air pollution? (α=0.05) **10**

10. The police plans to enforce speed limits by using radar traps at 4 different locations within the city limits. The radar traps at each of the locations L1, L2, L3 and L4 are operated 40%, 30%, 20%, and 30% of the time. If a person who is speeding on his way to work has probabilities of 0.2, 0.1, 0.5, and 0.2 respectively, of passing through these locations, what is the probability that he will receive a speeding ticket? Find also the probability that he will receive a speeding ticket at locations L1, L2, L3and L4. **10**

Bachelor Of Computer Application
(Bca - Revised)
Chapter 4: Term-End Examination, December 2015
Bcs - 040: Statistical Techniques

Time: 2 Hours
Maximum Marks: 50
Note: (i) Attempt both Sections i.e. Section A and Section B.
(ii) Attempt any four questions from Section A.
(iii) Attempt any three questions from Section B.
(iv) Use of Non-scientific calculator is allowed.

Section A

1. Write any two merits and demerits of Arithmetic Mean. Given below is the data about the number of seeds in a pod of a certain plant. Find the variance. **5**

No of Seeds	1	2	3	4	5	6
Frequency	8	14	7	12	3	1

2. Division A and B in a school have 20 students each. One student is to be selected from each division. What is the probability that Rahul in division A will be selected, if 2 students are selected out of 40 students? **5**

3. A die is rolled 1200 times with the following results:

No. that comes up	1	2	3	4	5	6
Frequency	195	289	202	242	163	109

Test if the die is unbiased at a 5% level of significance. (Given that $\chi_{0.05}(5) = 11.07$) **5**

4. Define simple random sampling. Describe the limitations of simple random sampling. Differentiate between SRSWR and SRSWOR methods of simple random sampling. **5**

5. Cancer is present in 22% of a population and is not present in the remaining 78%. An imperfect clinical test successfully detects the disease with a probability of 0.70. Thus, if a person has the disease in the serious form, the probability is 0.70 that the test will be positive and it is 0.30 if the test is negative. Moreover, among the unaffected persons, the probability that the test will be positive is 0.05. A person selected at random from the population is given the test and the result is positive. What is the probability that this person has cancer? **5**

6. The probability that Meena is on time to catch the bus to her office is 0.8. Find the probability that she is late
(a) exactly twice in a 6-day week, and
(b) at least once in a 6-day week. **5**

Section B

7. In a partially destroyed laboratory, record of an analysis of correlation of data, only the following results are legible:
Variance of x = 9. Regression equations:
(i) $8x - 10y + 66 = 0$
(ii) $40x - 18y - 214 = 0$
What were:
(a) the means of x and y,

(b) the coefficient of correlation between x and y,

(c) the standard deviation of y? **10**

8. The following table shows the sample values of 3 independent normal random variables, X_1, X_2, and X_3. Assuming that they have equal variances, test the hypothesis that they have the same mean by using ANOVA. (Given F (2, 9) (0.05) = 4.26) **10**

$$X_1 : 13 \quad 11 \quad 16 \quad 22$$
$$X_2 : 16 \quad 08 \quad 21 \quad 11$$
$$X_3 : 15 \quad 12 \quad 25 \quad 10$$

9. The following table gives, for a sample of married women, the level of education and marriage adjustment score:

Level of Education	Marriage	Adjustment	Score
Middle School	25	50	120
High School	05	30	60
College	10	40	60

Can you conclude from the above that the higher the level of education, the greater is the degree of adjustment in marriage? (Given x^2 (4, 0.05) = 9.488) **10**

10. A population of size 500 is divided into 4 strata. The following table gives the data on size and standard deviation of each stratum:

Strata	Size	Standard Deviation
I	100	05
II	150	08
III	150	07
IV	100	10

A stratified random sample of size 100 is to be drawn from the population. Determine the size of samples from each of these strata for:

(a) Proportional Allocation,

(b) Neyman's Optimum Allocation. **10**

Bachelor Of Computer Application
(Bca - Revised)
Chapter 5: Term-End Examination, June 2016
Bcs - 040: Statistical Techniques

Time: 2 Hours
Maximum Marks: 50
Note: (i) Attempt both Sections i.e., Section A and Section B.
(ii) Attempt any four questions from Section A.
(iii) Attempt any three questions from Section B.
(iv) Use of Non-scientific calculator is allowed.

Section A

1. The mean and standard deviation of 20 items is found to be 10 and 2, respectively. At the time of checking, it was found that one noted item with a value of 8 was incorrect. Calculate the mean and standard deviation if the wrong item is deleted. **5**

2. Let x_1 and x_2 be two independent random variables with variances $Var(x_1) = k$, $Var(x_2) = 2$. If the variance of $y = 3x_2 - x_1$ is 25, then find k. **5**

3. (a) State and prove the Addition theorem of probability. **2**
(b) Suppose that A and B are two independent events, associated with a random experiment. The probability of occurrence of event A or B is 0.8, while the probability of occurrence of event A is 0.5. Determine the probability of occurrence of event B. **3**

4. (a) What do you understand by a random variable? Define the types of random variables. **2**
(b) A bag contains 10 white and 3 black balls. Balls are drawn one by one without replacement till all the black balls are drawn. Find the probability that all black balls are drawn by the 6th draw. **3**

5. A survey of 64 medical labs revealed that the mean price charged for a certain test was ₹120, with a standard deviation of ₹60. Test whether the data indicates that the mean price of this test is more than ₹100 at a 5% level of significance. **5**

Section B

6. Describe the following tests in detail: **10**
(a) Paired t-test
(b) Chi-Square test for independence of attributes

7. Differentiate between any two of the following: **10**
(a) Simple Random Sampling With Replacement and Simple Random Sampling Without Replacement
(b) Probability (Random) Sampling and Non-Random Sampling
(c) One-Sample Test and Two-Sample Test

8. The following table shows the sample values of 3 independent normal random variables. Test whether they have the same mean using ANOVA. Given $F_{0.05}(2,9) = 4.26$. **10**

X_1	X_2	X_3
13	16	15
11	08	12
16	21	25

22	11	10

9. (a) Discuss the following: **4**

(i) Control chart for variables

(ii) Control chart for attributes

(b) Describe the control chart for $\bar{X}$ and R in detail. Also, suggest when RRR-chart and SSS-chart can be used.

5 + 1

Bachelor Of Computer Application
(Bca - Revised)

Chapter 6: Term-End Examination, December 2016

Bcs - 040: Statistical Techniques

Time: 2 Hours
Maximum Marks: 50
Note: (i) Attempt both Sections i.e., Section A and Section B.
(ii) Attempt any four questions from Section A.
(iii) Attempt any three questions from Section B.
(iv) Use of Non-scientific calculator is allowed.

Section A

1. Calculate the mean and standard deviation for the following data: **5**

Marks	Number of Students
0 - 10	8
10 - 20	8
20 - 30	10
30 - 40	36
40 - 50	12
50 - 60	17
60 - 70	10

2. Find the correlation coefficient between two variables X and Y and the slope of the regression line Y on X (i.e., b_{YX}). The observations on 20 pairs are as follows: **5**

$$\sum_{i=1}^{20} x_i = 15,\ \sum_{i=1}^{20} y_i = -6\ ,\ \sum_{i=1}^{20} x_i\, y_i = 50$$
$$\sum_{i=1}^{20} x_i^2 = 61\ ,\ \sum_{i=1}^{20} y_i^2 = 90$$

3. Box XXX contains 5 red and 4 blue balls. Box YYY contains 2 red and 5 blue balls. A ball is drawn at random from each box. Find the probability of drawing one red and one blue ball. **5**

4. Suppose 2% of the items made in a factory are defective. Find the probability that there are: **5**
(a) 3 defective items in a sample of 100, and
(b) no defective item in a sample of 50.

5. Define time series and describe its components briefly, with examples. **5**

Section B

6. Describe the following tests in detail: **10**
(a) Chi-square test for Goodness of fit
(b) F-test for Equality of two variances

7. Differentiate between any two of the following: **10**
(a) Neyman Allocation and Optimum Allocation
(b) Correlation and Regression
(c) Random Sampling and Non-Random Sampling

8. The sales figures of a company are given below. Compute the moving averages for the lengths of 4 and 2 separately. **10**

Day	Sales
1	230
2	200
3	250
4	300
5	200
6	225
7	400
8	450
9	415
10	420
11	500
12	300
13	400
14	300
15	315

9. A die is rolled 1200 times with the following results: **10**

Number on Die	Frequency
1	195
2	289
3	202
4	242
5	163
6	109

Test if the die is unbiased at a 5% level of significance.

Bachelor Of Computer Application
(Bca - Revised)
Chapter 7: Term-End Examination, June 2017
Bcs - 040: Statistical Techniques

Time: 2 Hours
Maximum Marks: 50
Note: (i) Attempt both Sections i.e. Section A and Section B.
(ii) Attempt any four questions from Section A.
(iii) Attempt any three questions from Section B.
(iv) Use of Non-scientific calculator is allowed.

Section A

1. Data of rainfall were collected to study the rainfall patterns in 50 different areas of a state and are given in the following table: **5**

166 154 168 217 199 168 205 201 173
192 157 224 160 209 203 182 182 151
191 188 226 176 228 182 228 186 229
219 220 189 188 179 199 150 190 215
207 211 228 204 195 221 206 215 218
168 183 213 180 208

Construct the continuous frequency distribution by considering intervals 150–160, 160–170, 170–180, etc. Also, draw a Histogram. **5**

2. The chances of catching cold by workers working in an ice factory during winter are 25%. What is the probability that out of 5 workers, 4 or more will catch a cold? **5**

3. A quality controller selected 50 laptops from the production line each day over a period of 10 days to monitor the manufacturing process. Fifty laptops were inspected for defectives and the number of defective laptops found each day was recorded and given in the following table: **5**

Day	1	2	3	4	5	6	7	8	9	10
No. of defective laptops	3	4	4	10	4	2	4	5	6	2

4. Construct a suitable control chart and interpret the results.
(a) Differentiate between estimator and estimate with examples. **2**
(b) A manager of a bulb manufacturing company tests a random sample of 100 bulbs and determined the average life to be 300 hours and standard deviation 50 hours. Obtain the 99% confidence interval for the average life of the bulbs. (Given that $Z_{0.005} = 2.58$) **3**

5. (a) Distinguish between random sampling and non-random sampling. **2**
(b) The monthly income (in thousands) of five workers in a small company is as follows:
25, 20, 30, 15, 10. How many samples of size 2 are possible if we select the samples without replacement? Write all of them. **3**

6. A computer chip manufacturer claims that at most 2% of the chips it produces are defective. To check the claim of the manufacturer, a researcher selects a sample of 250 of these chips. If there are eight defective chips among these 250, test the null hypothesis that more than 2% of the chips are defective at a 5% level of significance. Does this disprove the manufacturer's claim?

(Given that $Z_{0.05} = 1.645$) **5**

Section B

7. (a) What is time series? Explain briefly the components of the time series with examples. **4**

(b) In a company, cases of CPUs are manufactured, and the production for ten years is given below: **6**

Year	Production (in 1000 tonnes)
2001	26
2002	27
2003	28
2004	30
2005	29
2006	27
2007	30
2008	31
2009	32
2010	31

Determine the (i) 3-yearly, and (ii) 4-yearly centered moving averages.

8. A researcher wants to compare the waiting time of three hospitals (A, B, and C). The time measured from the instant the patient arrives in the emergency room until the patient is attended to by a doctor is recorded in the following table: **10**

Waiting time (in minutes)

Hospital A	Hospital B	Hospital C
8	2	10
4	4	2
3	3	9
6	5	5
3	7	
6		

(Given that $F_{0.05,2,12} = 3.89$)

Is there enough evidence that the average waiting times for a patient to meet a doctor in these hospitals are equal at a 5% level of significance?

9. A company manufactures pipes of small diameter. Four observations of the diameters of the pipes were taken periodically. The following table gives the values of four observations taken 10 times during a working day: **10**

Sample No.	I	II	III	IV
1	4.1	4.3	4.2	4.2
2	4.3	4.1	4.3	4.5
3	4.2	4.3	4.4	4.3
4	4.1	4.2	4.4	4.1
5	4.3	4.1	4.2	4.2
6	4	4.2	4.1	4.1
7	4	4.5	4.2	4.1
8	4.2	4.3	4.1	4.2
9	4.4	4.2	4.1	4.5
10	4.4	4.2	4.3	4.3

Calculate the control limits for the mean and range. (Given that $A_2 = 0.729, D_3 = 0, D_4 = 2.282$)

10. The table given below shows the relation between the performances of students in Statistics and Computer Sciences. Test the hypothesis that the performance in Statistics is independent of the performance in Computer Sciences using a 5% level of significance.

(Given that $x_{0.05,4}{}^2 = 9.49$) **10**

	High Grade	**Medium Grade**	**Low Grade**
High Grade	36	72	42
Medium Grade	34	122	44
Low Grade	50	56	44

Bachelor Of Computer Application
(Bca - Revised)
Chapter 8: Term-End Examination, December 2017
Bcs - 040: Statistical Techniques

Time: 2 Hours
Maximum Marks: 50
Note: (i) Attempt both Sections i.e., Section A and Section B.
(ii) Attempt any four questions from Section A.
(iii) Attempt any three questions from Section B.
(iv) Use of Non-scientific calculator is allowed.

Section A

1. A research was conducted to improve the safety plans in a factory. In this study, the accidental data of the factory for the last 50 weeks were compiled. These data are grouped into the frequency distribution as shown below:

Number of Accidents	Number of Weeks
0 — 5	28
5 — 10	22
10 —15	10
15 — 20	6
20 — 25	2

Draw a histogram and calculate the average number of accidents per week. **5**

2. A cricket ball manufacturing company wants to check the variation in the weight of the balls. For this, 25 samples each of size 4, are selected and the weight of each ball is measured (in grams). The sum of the sample averages and the sum of sample ranges were found to be $\sum_{i=1}^{25} \bar{x}_i = 4010$ grams and $\sum_{i=1}^{25} R_i = 72$ grams, respectively. Compute the control limits for the $\bar{X}$ and R-charts. It is given that $A_2 = 0.729, D_3 = 0 \; and \; D_4 = 2.282$. **5**

3. An insurance company insured 1000 scooter drivers, 3000 car drivers, and 6000 truck drivers. The probabilities that the scooter, car, and truck drivers meet with an accident are 0.2, 0.04, and 0.25, respectively. One of the insured persons meets with an accident. What is the probability that he is a car driver? **5**

4. A researcher would like to test whether there is any significant difference between the proportion of safety consciousness of men and women while driving a car. In a sample of 300 men, 130 said that they used seat belts. In a sample of 300 women, 90 said that they used seat belts. Test the claim that there is no significant difference between the proportion of safety consciousness of men and women while driving a car at a 5% level of significance. (Given that $Z_{0.025} = 1.96$) **5**

5. A company manufactures two types of bulbs, (A and B). The manager of the company tests a random sample of 50 bulbs of type A and 60 bulbs of type B and obtains the following information:

Mean Life (in hours)	Standard Deviation (in hours)
Type A: 1300	50
Type B: 1200	60

Obtain a 99% confidence interval for the difference in the average life of the two types of bulbs.
(Given that $Z_{0.025} = 2.58$) **5**

6. (a) Differentiate between parametric and non-parametric tests.

(b) A washing machine company chooses a random sample of 10 motors received from one of the suppliers. It determines the length of life of each of the motors. The results (in thousands of hours) are as follows:

4.5, 5.0, 4.2, 4.8, 4.2, 5.1, 4.0, 4.2, 4.2, 4.5

Compute a point estimate of the mean length of life of the motors received from the supplier. **5**

Section B

7. A steel rod is subjected to stress. The tensile strength of the rod at different values of stress is recorded. Find a relation between the tensile strength and the stress. The data is given below:

Stress (kg)	Tensile strength (m/kg)
10	6
9	3
7	2
8	4
11	5

Also, predict the tensile strength at a stress of 5 kg. **10**

8. A computer engineer identifies four ways that a certain job can be done. To determine how long it takes operators to do the job when each of these methods is used, the engineer asks four operators to do the job using method A, another four operators to do the job using method B, and so on. Each operator's time (in seconds) is shown below:

A	B	C	D
19	18	21	22
17	16	20	23
22	15	19	21
20	14	19	20

Construct the relevant analysis of variance table and test the hypothesis that the average time of all operators is equal at a 1% level of significance. (Given that $F_{0.01,(3,12)} = 5.95$) **10**

9. The following contingency table presents the analysis of 300 persons according to hair color and eye color:

	Eye Colour		
Hair Colour	Blue	Grey	Brown
Fair	30	10	40
Brown	40	20	40
Black	50	30	40

Test the hypothesis that there is an association between hair color and eye color at a 5% level of significance. (Given that $x^2{}_{0.05,4} = 9.49$) **10**

10. (a) Distinguish between random sampling and non-random sampling.
(b) Suppose an analyst studies three villages having populations $N_1 = 50000, N_2 = 30000,$ $and\ N_3 = 40000$ respectively. A stratified random sample is to be taken with a total sample size of n = 500. Determine the sample size to be selected from each village individually using the method of:
(i) proportional allocation
(ii) optimal allocation.
From the previous survey, it is known that the standard deviations are $S_1 = 30, S_2 = 15, and\ S_3 = 20.$ **10**

Bachelor Of Computer Application
(Bca - Revised)
Chapter 9: Term-End Examination, June 2018
Bcs - 040: Statistical Techniques

Time: 2 Hours
Maximum Marks: 50
Note: (i) Attempt both Sections i.e. Section A and Section B.
(ii) Attempt any four questions from Section A.
(iii) Attempt any three questions from Section B.
(iv) Use of Non-scientific calculator is allowed.

SECTION A

1. Draw a histogram and a frequency polygon for the following data. Also, find its mean. Further, comment on the shape of the distribution.

Time (in minutes)	No. of Machines
20 — 25	03
25 — 30	07
30 — 35	11
35 — 40	08
40 — 45	05
45 — 50	02

5

2. A sample of size 3 is to be selected from a population of 10 households. List all possible samples by (a) Linear systematic; (b) Circular systematic sampling. **5**

3. A bag contains 10 white and 3 black balls. Balls are drawn one by one without replacement till all the black balls are drawn. Find the probability that this procedure comes to an end at the 6th draw. **5**

4. From a list of 500 names and addresses, 100 names were selected without replacement and 25 wrong addresses were found. Identify the population and estimate the total number of addresses required to be corrected in the list. Also, estimate the standard error. **5**

5. In order to find the correlation coefficient between two variables X and Y from 20 pairs of observations, the following calculations were made:

$\sum X=15, \sum Y=-6, \sum XY=50, \sum X2=61$, and $\sum Y2=90$.

Calculate the correlation coefficient and the slope of the regression line of Y on X. **5**

6. A random sample of size 10 from a normal population gives the values 64, 72, 65, 70, 68, 71, 65, 62, 66, 67. If it is known that the standard error of the sample mean is $\sqrt{0.64}$, find the 95% confidence limits for the population mean. Also, find the population variance. **5**

Section B

7. (a) The police plans to enforce speed limits by using radar traps at 4 different locations within the city limits. The radar traps at each of the locations L1, L2, L3, and L4 are operated 40%, 30%, 20%, and 10% of the time spectively. If a person who is speeding on his way to work has probabilities 0.2, 0.1, 0.5, and 0.2 respectively, of passing through these locations, what is the probability that he will receive a speeding ticket? Also, find the probability that he will receive a speeding ticket at location L1. **5**

(b) Explain the exponential smoothing method. Use the same to forecast the following data. Also, estimate the error. [Take W=0.1] **5**

Table: Number of new colleges opened in the country

Year	Colleges
2001	5
2002	3
2003	3
2004	4
2005	3
2006	6
2007	4

8. The result of a survey regarding radio listeners' preference for different types of music is given in the following table with listeners classified by age group:

Types of Music Preferred	**Age Group**		
	19 — 25	26 — 35	Above 35
National Music	60	60	30
Foreign Music	190	264	96
Indifferent	50	76	74

Test at a 5% level of significance whether the type of music is dependent on the age group. (Given that $x^2{}_{4,5\%}$=9.488) **10**

9. A company wants to test whether its 3 salesmen (A, B, and C) have the same selling ability.Their records of sales (in '000) during various weeks of the last month are given below:

Salesman	**Week 1**	**Week 2**	**Week 3**	**Week 4**
A	16	20	18	25
B	22	20	15	26
C	25	24	16	20

Prepare a one-way ANOVA table and test the hypothesis that all the salesmen perform equally over the week. (Given $F_{5\%}$,(2,9)=4.26) **10**

10. Write short notes on any four of the following: **4*2(1/2)=10**
(a) Cluster Sampling
(b) Stratified Sampling
(c) Control Charts
(d) Goodness of Fit
(e) Moving Average

Bachelor Of Computer Application
(Bca - Revised)
Chapter 10: Term-End Examination, December 2018
Bcs-040: Statistical Techniques

Time: 2 Hours
Maximum Marks: 50
Note:
Attempt both Section A and Section B.
Attempt any four questions from Section A.
Attempt any three questions from Section B.

Section A

1. The mean and standard deviation of 20 items is found to be 10 and 2, respectively. At the time of checking, it was found that one item with value 8 was incorrect. Calculate the mean and standard deviation if the wrong item is omitted. **5**

2. A population consists of the numbers 2, 5, 7, 8, and 10. Write all possible simple random samples of size 3 (without replacement). Verify that the sample mean is an unbiased estimator of the population mean. **5**

3. A random sample of 10 males from a normal population showed a mean height of 66 inches, and the sum of squares from this mean is equal to 90 square inches. Is it reasonable to believe that the average height is greater than 64 inches? Justify your answer at a 5% level of significance. (Use $t_{0.05}$ (9) =2.26) **5**

4. Write short notes on any two of the following:
(a) Simple Random Sampling
(b) Systematic Sampling
(c) Stratified Sampling **2.5 x 2 = 5**

5. A random sample of size 64 has been drawn from a population with standard deviation 20. The mean of the sample is 80.
(a) Calculate 95% confidence limits for the population mean.
(b) How does the width of the confidence interval change if the sample size is 256 instead? **5**

6. Box A contains 5 red and 4 blue balls, and Box B contains 2 red and 5 blue balls. A ball is drawn at random from each box. Find the probability that one is red and the other is blue. **5**

Section B

7. The following table gives data for a sample of married women, the level of education, and marriage adjustment score:

	Marriage Adjustment Score		
Level of Education	**Low**	**High**	**Very High**
Middle School	25	5	10
High School	50	30	40
College	120	60	60

Can you conclude from the above that the higher the level of education, the greater the djustment in marriage? Justify your answer.
Given that ${x^2}_{0.05}(4)$=9.488. **10**

8. Refill of cartons with apple juice is taking place in a plant. Data for 14 days was collected, and 100 cartons were checked every day for proper filling. Data is as given below:

S. No.	X
1	8
2	2
3	4
4	1
5	3
6	3
7	2
8	4
9	9
10	7
11	6
12	8
13	5
14	9

Compute the UCL, LCL, and CL using an appropriate control chart. Also, draw the chart. **10**

9. Plot the following data about demand for an item. Find the centered moving averages by taking n=3. Use these to forecast the next two months' demand. **10**

Month	Demand
1	46
2	56
3	54
4	43
5	57
6	56
7	67
8	62
9	50
10	56
11	47
12	56

10. The following table gives the yield of a hybrid variety of wheat in quintals per acre from 17 trial plots of land treated with four types of fertilizers:

Treatment with Fertilizers

A	B	C	D
24	31	39	38
39	25	41	32
35	26	33	35
	21	40	34
		45	26

Use ANOVA to test whether the effect of fertilizers differs in terms of average yields.
Given that $F_{0.05}(3,13) = 3.41$ **10**

Bachelor Of Computer Application
(Bca - Revised)
Chapter 11: Term Examination, June 2019
Bcs-040: Statistical Techniques

Time: 2 Hours
Maximum Marks: 50
Note:

Attempt both sections, i.e., Section A and Section B.
Attempt any four questions from Section A.
Attempt any three questions from Section B.
Non-scientific calculator is allowed.

Section A

1. The following table represents the daily wages (in rupees) of the workers in a certain commercial organization:

Daily Wages (in ₹)	**200–300**	**300–400**	**400–500**	**500–600**
Number of Workers	5	10	3	2

Calculate the mean and standard deviation of the above data. **5**

2. A person is known to hit a target in 4 out of 5 shots, whereas another person is known to hit the target in 2 out of 3 shots. Find the probability that the target is hit when they both try. **5**

3. An oil exploration firm plans to drill four holes. It is assumed that the probability of oil yield from each hole is 1/5. Since the holes are in quite different locations, the outcome of drilling one hole is statistically independent of the outcome of drilling any other hole. What is the probability that two or more holes produce oil? **5**

4. A population of five households has the following monthly incomes (in thousand rupees):

Household	**1**	**2**	**3**	**4**	**5**
Income (₹)	14	10	12	20	18

Write all possible samples of size 2 without replacement and show that the sample mean gives an unbiased estimate of the population mean. **5**

5. Explain any two of the following: **5**
(a) Z-test for mean
(b) Paired t-test
(c) Simple random sampling

Section B

6. An investigator is interested to know the level of knowledge about the history of India among three different schools in a city. A test is given to four students of class 8 in each school. Their scores out of 10 are given below:

I	**II**	**III**
8	6	6
6	4	5
7	6	5
5	5	6

Test the equality of the average scores of the three schools at the 5% level of significance.
Given $F_{(2,9)}5\% = 3.41$. **10**

7. A manager of a car company wants to estimate the relationship between the age of cars and their annual maintenance cost. The following data from six cars of the same model are obtained:

Age of Car (in years)	**1**	**2**	**3**	**4**	**5**	**6**
Annual Maintenance Cost (in ₹100)	10	15	18	20	25	35

(a) Construct a scatter diagram for the data.
(b) Fit the best linear regression line, taking the annual maintenance cost as the dependent variable and the age of the car as the independent variable.
(c) Use this regression line to predict the annual maintenance cost for a car aged 8 years. **2 + 7 + 1**

8. The following contingency table presents the analysis of 300 persons according to hair color and eye color:

Hair Color	**Eye Color**			**Total**
	Blue	Grey	Brown	
Fair	30	10	40	80
Brown	40	20	40	100
Black	50	30	40	120
Total	120	60	120	300

Test the hypothesis that there is an association between hair color and eye color at the 1% level of significance. Given $x^2{}_{(4),1\%}$=13.28 , $x^2{}_{(6),1\%} = 16.81$. **10**

9. (a) Define stratified random sampling.
(b) Suppose an analyst studies three villages having populations $N_1 = 50000, N_2 = 30000, and\ N_3 = 40000$ respectively. A stratified random sample is to be taken with a total sample size of n = 500. Determine the sample size to be selected from each village individually using the method of:
(i) proportional allocation
(ii) optimal allocation.
From the previous survey, it is known that the standard deviations are $S_1 = 30, S_2 = 15,\ and\ S_3 = 20$. **10**

Bachelor Of Computer Application
(Bca - Revised)
Chapter 12: Term Examination, December 2019
Bcs-040: Statistical Techniques

Time: 2 Hours
Maximum Marks: 50
Note:

Attempt both sections, i.e., Section A and Section B.
Attempt any four questions from Section A.
Attempt any three questions from Section B.
Non-scientific calculator is allowed.

Section A

1. The marks obtained by 25 BCA students in a statistical techniques paper out of 50 are given below:

48 10 18 02 27 23 17 23 34 35
35 37 42 37 22 42 24 26 40 08
25 13 20 23 35

(a) Present the above data in the form of a continuous frequency distribution by taking the first class interval as (0-10). **2**

(b) Prepare a histogram of the obtained distribution. **3**

2. The following table gives daily wages (in rupees) of workers in a certain commercial organization:

Daily Wages (in ₹)	**200–300**	**300–400**	**400–500**	**500–600**	**600–700**
Number of Workers	10	12	20	5	3

Calculate the median wages of the workers. **5**

3. A problem of statistics is given to three students A, B, and C whose chances of solving it are 0.3, 0.5, and 0.6 respectively. What is the probability that the problem will be solved? **5**

4. The probability distribution of a discrete random variable XXX is as follows: **2+3**

X	**0**	**1**	**2**	**3**	**4**	**5**
p(X)	0	C	C	2C	3C	C

(a) Find the constant C.
(b) Find $P(X<3)$.

5. A filling machine is set to pour 952 ml of oil into bottles. The filled amount is normally distributed with a mean of 952 ml and a standard deviation of 4 ml. Find the probability that a bottle contains oil between 952 ml and 956 ml. (Given $P(0 \leq z \leq 1)=0.3413$) **5**

Section B

7. Explain any two of the following: **5+5**
(a) Criteria for a good estimator

(b) Stratified random sampling
(c) Systematic random sampling

8. Three salesmen were posted in different areas of a company. The number of units sold by them is given below:

A	B	C
10	12	5
7	8	10
9	5	6
10	7	5

On the basis of the above information, can it be concluded that there is a significant difference in the performance of the salesmen at the 5% level of significance?
(Given $F_{(2,9)}5\%=4.26$) **10**

9. 1000 students at the college level were graded according to their IQ level and economic condition of their parents. The data are as follows:

Economic Condition	**IQ Level**	
	High	Low
Poor	240	160
Rich	460	140

Test whether the IQ level of students is independent of the economic condition of their parents at the 1% level of significance.
(Given $x^2{}_{(4),1\%}=13.28$) **10**

10. The pulse rate of 6 people was recorded before and after taking a new drug. The obtained pulse rates are given below:

Before	68	71	84	93	67	74
After	71	70	81	97	73	80

Can it be concluded that there is a significant increase in the pulse rate at the 5% level of significance after consuming the new drug? (Given $t_{(5),5\%}=2.015$, $t_{(6),5\%}= 1.943$) **10**

Bachelor Of Computer Application
(Bca - Revised)
Chapter 13: Term Examination, June 2020
Bcs-040: Statistical Techniques

Time: 2 Hours
Maximum Marks: 50
Note:

Attempt both sections, i.e., Section A and Section B.
Attempt any four questions from Section A.
Attempt any three questions from Section B.
Non-scientific calculator is allowed.

Section A

1. Given the following sample of 20 numbers:
12, 41, 48, 58, 14, 43, 50, 59, 15, 45, 52, 72, 18, 45, 54, 78, 41, 47, 56, 79
(i) Compute the mean, variance, and standard deviation.
(ii) If the largest value in the sample of 20 numbers is changed to 500, how will the mean and variance change? Justify your answer. **5**

2. A dice is rolled 1200 times with the following results:

Number that comes up	1	2	3	4	5	6
Frequency	195	289	202	242	163	109

Test the hypothesis that the dice is unbiased at a 5% level of significance.
(Given $x^2{}_{0.05}(5)$=11.07) **5**

3. Calls at a telephone switchboard occur at an average rate of 6 calls per 10 minutes. Suppose the operator leaves for a 5-minute coffee break. What is the probability that exactly two calls occur while the operator is away? **5**

4. Fit a linear trend y=a+b* (Demand) to the data collected from an umbrella manufacturing unit: **5**

Month	**1**	**2**	**3**	**4**	**5**	**6**
Demand	46	56	54	43	57	56

5. Construct an ANOVA table for one-way classification. **5**

6. Briefly discuss any two of the following: **5**
(i) Goodness of fit test
(ii) Binomial distribution
(iii) t-test for mean

Section B

7. In a partially destroyed laboratory, the legible record for correlation analysis of data is preserved as follows:
(a) Variance of x=9
(b) Regression equations:
i. 8x−10y+66=0

ii. $40x-18y-214=0$

Analyze the preserved records and determine:

(i) The mean of x and y.

(ii) The coefficient of correlation between x and y.

(iii) The standard deviation of y. **10**

8. The following table shows the sample values of 3 independent normal random variables X1, X2, and X3. Assuming that they have equal variance, test the hypothesis that they have the same mean using ANOVA (Given $F_{(2,9)}(0.05) = 4.26$): **10**

X1	13	11	16	22
X2	16	8	21	11
X3	15	12	25	10

9. What do you understand by the term "Time Series"? Discuss all the categories into which Time Series is classified. **10**

10. Discuss the term "Systematic Sampling." Differentiate between linear and circular systematic sampling. Give two advantages and limitations of systematic sampling. **10**

Bachelor Of Computer Application
(Bca - Revised)
Chapter 14: Term Examination, December 2020
Bcs-040: Statistical Techniques

Time: 2 Hours
Maximum Marks: 50
Note:

Attempt both sections, i.e., Section A and Section B.
Attempt any four questions from Section A.
Attempt any three questions from Section B.
Use of non-scientific calculator is allowed.

Section A

1. Calculate the correlation coefficient and the slope of the regression line Y on X, using the data given below:

$\Sigma x=15$, $\Sigma y=-6$, $\Sigma xy=50$, $\Sigma x^2=61$, $\Sigma y^2=90$

The above data is calculated from 20 pairs of observations for variables X and Y. **5**

2. Suppose A and B are two independent events associated with a random experiment. If the probability of occurrence of either A or B is 0.6, and the probability that only A occurs is 0.4, determine the probability of occurrence of event B. **5**

3. Suppose 2% of the items made in a factory are defective. Find the probability that there are:
(i) 3 defectives in a sample of 100
(ii) No defectives in a sample of 50 **5**

4. The mean weekly sales of chocolate packets in different departmental stores were 146.3 packets per store. After an advertisement campaign, the mean weekly sales of 22 stores for a typical week increased to 153.7 and showed a standard deviation of 17.2. Was the advertisement campaign successful at a 5% level of significance?

(Given $t_{(21),0.05}=2.08$) **5**

5. Differentiate between the following:
(i) Parametric and Non-parametric tests
(ii) Binomial distribution and Poisson distribution **5**

6. An incomplete frequency distribution is given below:

Class Interval	Frequency
10–20	12
20–30	30
30–40	?
40–50	65
50–60	?
60–70	25
70–80	18

Given that the median value of 200 observations is 46, determine the missing frequencies using the median formula. **5**

Section B

7. Using the regression line $\hat{y} = 90 + 50x$, fill in the missing values in the table below:

Sample No. (i)	12	21	15	1	24
x_i	0.96	1.28	1.65	1.84	2.35
y_i	138	160	178	190	210
$\hat{y}_i$	138	—	—	—	—
$e_i = y_i - \hat{y}_i$	0	—	—	—	—

After filling the table, compute the parameters R and R^2. Interpret the correlation between X and Y. **10**

8. A chemical firm wants to determine how four catalysts (i.e., 1, 2, 3, and 4) differ in their yields. The firm conducted the experiment in three of its plants (i.e., A, B, and C). In each plant, the yield is measured with each catalyst. The yield (in quintals) is tabulated below: **10**

Plant	Catalyst 1	Catalyst 2	Catalyst 3	Catalyst 4
A	2	1	2	4
B	3	2	1	3
C	1	3	3	1

Perform an ANOVA and comment on whether the yield due to a particular catalyst is significant or not at a 5% level of significance. (Given $F_{(3,6)}$=4.76) **10**

9. What do you understand by the term 'Forecasting'? How does forecasting differ from prediction? Give suitable examples in support of your answer. Briefly discuss the. forecasting models. **10**

10. Telephone directories have telephone numbers which are combinations of ten digits (0 to 9). An observer notes the frequency of occurrence of these digits and wants to test whether the digits occur with the same frequency. The data is tabulated below:

Digit	0	1	2	3	4	5	6	7	8	9
Freq	99	100	82	65	50	77	88	57	82	30

Test the hypothesis that the digits occur with the same frequency at α=0.05.
(Given $\chi_9^2(0.05)$=16.918) **10**

Bachelor Of Computer Application
(Bca - Revised)
Chapter 15: Term Examination, June 2021
Bcs-040: Statistical Techniques

Time: 2 Hours
Maximum Marks: 50
Note:

Attempt both sections, i.e., Section A and Section B.
Attempt any four questions from Section A.
Attempt any three questions from Section B.
Use of non-scientific calculator is allowed.

Section A

1. An Automobile service center performed the following number of car services each month:
15, 18, 25, 40, 25, 18, 25, 21, 30, 33, 25, 20, 10, 28, 36, 15, 26, 35, 20, 21, 32, 40, 32, 16, 12, 14, 22, 26, 37, 16.
(i) Construct a continuous frequency distribution of the above data by taking a suitable class width.
(ii) Draw the histogram of the constructed continuous frequency distribution in part (i). **5**

2. The information regarding the production of wheat (in thousand kg) in 25 districts is collected for a particular season. Select a possible systematic random sample of 7 units from the data given below:
23, 20, 30, 37, 76, 36, 13, 36, 16, 58, 53, 83, 10, 15, 13, 17, 12, 16, 17, 21, 20, 18, 61, 31, 71.
Also, calculate the sample mean from the selected units. **5**

3. A shopkeeper claims that the average life of a CFL bulb is 1600 hours. To check this claim, a researcher takes a sample of 100 CFL bulbs of the same make randomly and finds a mean lifetime of 1570 hours with a standard deviation of 120 hours. Is the claim acceptable at a 5% level of significance? (Given that $Z=\pm1.96$) **5**

4. The incidence of occupational disease in an industry is such that the workers have a 20% chance of suffering from it. What is the probability that out of six workers:
(i) Four or more will contract the disease?
(ii) Three will contract the disease? **5**

5. Differentiate between the following with one example of each:
(i) Assignable causes and chance causes
(ii) Producer's risk and consumer's risk **5**

6. Use a moving average of length 3 for the data on sales given in the following table:

Month	Sales
1	25
2	15
3	30
4	38
5	58
6	62
7	85
8	88
9	60
10	40

11	40
12	38

Calculate the moving average and plot it against the appropriate month. Also, plot the data on the same graph. **5**

Section B

7. A researcher wishes to test whether a person's cholesterol level will change if the diet is changed. She takes a sample of 15 persons and divides them into 3 diet groups randomly. The data of cholesterol levels (in mg/deciliter) for the three groups are given below:

Cholesterol Levels	Diet 1	Diet 2	Diet 3
	190	210	170
	170	200	200
	210	230	210
	180	210	200
	200	190	205

Test whether the average effect of different diets on cholesterol levels differs significantly at a 5% level of significance. (Given that $F_{(2,12)}(0.05)=3.885$) **10**

8. The following contingency table presents the analysis of 300 persons according to hair color and eye color:

Hair Color	Eye Color			Total
	Blue	Grey	Brown	
Burgundy	30	10	40	80
Brown	40	20	40	100
Black	50	30	40	120
Total	120	60	120	300

Test the hypothesis that there is an association between hair color and eye color at a 5% level of significance. (Given $\chi^2_{(0.05,4)}=9.49$) **10**

9. Determine a regression equation y=a+bx for the data given in the table below:

X	Y
1	2
1	3
2	5
3	6
4	8
4	8
5	9
6	10
6	9
7	11

Use the fitted regression line to predict y when x=8. Draw a scatter diagram to represent the data. **10**

10. Write short notes on any two of the following:
(i) Exponential smoothing method

(ii) Cluster sampling

(iii) Correlation and rank-correlation **5 x 2 = 10**

Bachelor Of Computer Application
(Bca - Revised)
Chapter 16: Term Examination, December 2021
Bcs-040: Statistical Techniques

Time: 2 Hours
Maximum Marks: 50
Note:

Attempt both sections, i.e., Section A and Section B.
Attempt any four questions from Section A.
Attempt any three questions from Section B.
Use of non-scientific calculator is allowed.

Section A

1. A pharmacologist measured the amount of dopamine (no. of moles/gm) in the brains of each of 10 rats. The observed data is given below:

6.8, 7.0, 5.3, 6.0, 5.9, 5.6, 6.8, 7.4, 6.2, 7.0

Calculate:
(i) The mean and standard deviation
(ii) Coefficient of variation **5**

2. In a certain population of women, 5% have breast cancer, 15% are smokers, and 3% are smokers as well as have breast cancer. A woman is selected at random from the population. What is the probability that she has breast cancer or she is a smoker? **5**

3. The pulse rate of 6 people was recorded before and after taking a new drug, which are given below:

	Pulse Rate					
Before	68	71	84	93	67	74
After	71	70	82	97	73	80

On the basis of the above information, can you conclude that there is a significant effect of the new drug to increase the pulse rate at 1% level of significance?
(Given $t_{5\,(0.01)}$=4.032) **5**

4. A company produces electric bulbs. To estimate the average life of the bulbs, the quality inspector selects 80 bulbs randomly. She finds that the average life of these bulbs is 50 hours. Find the population average life of the electric bulbs produced by the company using 95% confidence limits. **5**

5. The average yield of wheat crop (in quintals/ha) pertaining to fields of 40 villages in a district is given below:

20, 21, 32, 41, 55, 22, 64, 42, 28, 35, 25, 25, 24, 32, 75, 28, 29, 38, 19, 19, 16, 28, 30, 29, 29, 19, 37, 34, 31, 35, 29, 19, 27, 42, 39, 11, 26, 21, 45, 61.

Select a systematic random sample of 10 units and find the average of it. **5**

6. The yearly water consumption in a small city for ten years is given below. Determine the trend values by using a 3-yearly moving average. Also, plot the values and interpret the results: **5**

Year	Water Consumption (in thousand gallons)
2007	26
2008	27
2009	28

2010	30
2011	29
2012	27
2013	30
2014	31
2015	32
2016	31

Section B

7. Twenty individuals were randomly assigned to four different production processes. Production of units per hour for the four processes is given below:

Process	I	II	III	IV
	33	30	28	34
	30	35	38	28
	28	30	30	29
	29	38	34	26
	30	34	30	28

Determine if there is a significant difference in the average production units per hour for the four types of production processes.
(Given $F_{(3,16)(5\%)}$=5.24) **10**

8. A population of size 10,000 is divided into 4 strata. Their sizes and standard deviations are given below:

Strata	I	II	III	IV
N_i= Sizes	5000	1000	2000	2000
S_i	25	10	15	20

A stratified random sample of size 500 is to be drawn from this population. Determine the sizes of samples from these strata in case:
(i) Proportional allocation is used
(ii) Neyman's optimum allocation is used. **10**

9. 1000 students at the college level were graded according to their IQ levels and the economic condition of their parents, as follows:

Economic Condition	IQ Level	Total
	High	Low
Rich	230	170
Poor	470	130
Total	700	300

Test the hypothesis that IQ levels are independent of the economic conditions at 1% level of significance. (Given $\chi^2_{1\,(0.01)}$=6.63) **10**

10. A gynecologist recorded the blood pressure (BP) of her patients and collected the following data:

Age (in years)	BP (in mmHg)
23	65
24	60
25	62
26	70
28	70

29	73
31	75
35	83
40	90

Fit the regression line for the given data and estimate BP if the age of the patient is 38 years. **10**

Bachelor Of Computer Application
(BCA - Revised)
Chapter 17: Term Examination, June 2022
Bcs-040: Statistical Techniques

Time: 2 Hours
Maximum Marks: 50
Note:

Attempt both sections, i.e., Section A and Section B.
Attempt any four questions from Section A.
Attempt any three questions from Section B.
Use of non-scientific calculator is allowed.

Section A

1. A random sample of 50 students of mathematics taken from a total of 200, showed a mean of 75 and a standard deviation of 10. Find 95% confidence limits for the mean. (Given Z=1.96) **5**

2. Calculate the mean and standard deviation from the following data: **5**

Marks	No. of Students
0–10	10
10–20	9
20–30	25
30–40	30
40–50	16
50–60	10

3. In order to find the correlation coefficient between two variables X and Y from 20 pairs of observations, the following calculations were made:

$\Sigma x=15$, $\Sigma y=+6$, $\Sigma xy=50$, $\Sigma x^2=61$, $\Sigma y^2=90$

Calculate the correlation coefficient and the slope of the regression line of Y on X. **5**

4. Differentiate between Simple Random Sampling and Systematic Random Sampling. **5**

5. List the advantages and disadvantages of using a sampling approach instead of a census approach for studying the characteristics of data. **5**

Section B

6. Describe the following tests in detail:
(a) Time series and its components
(b) Chi-square test for independence of attributes **10**

7. (a) Compute the three-yearly moving average of the following data: **5**

Day	Sales
1	45
2	46
3	48

4	47
5	58
6	58
7	51
8	52
9	53
10	45
11	51
12	61

(b) An automobile tyre manufacturing company claims that the average life of a particular grade of tyre is more than 20,000 km when used under normal driving conditions. A random sample of 16 tyres was tested and mean and standard deviation of 22,000 km and 5,000 km respectively were calculated. Assuming the life of the tyres in km to be normally distributed, decide whether the manufacturer's claim is true. Use a 5% level of significance. (Given $t_{0.05,15}$=1.75) **5**

8. The following contingency table presents the analysis of 300 persons according to hair color and eye color:

Hair Color	**Eye Color**			**Total**
	Blue	Grey	Brown	
Fair	30	10	40	80
Brown	40	20	40	100
Black	50	30	40	120
Total	120	60	120	300 $\chi^2_{(0.05,4)}$=9.49)

Test the hypothesis that there is an association between hair color and eye color at the 5% level of significance. (Given that $\chi^2_{(0.05,4)}$=9.49) **10**

9. A computer engineer identifies A, B, and C as three methods to do a certain job. To determinehow long the operator takes to do the job when each of these methods is used, the engineer asks four operators to do the job using method A, another four operators to do the job using method B, and so on. Each operator's time (in minutes) is shown below:

A	B	C
19	18	21
17	16	20
22	15	19
20	14	19

Construct the relevant analysis of variance table and test the hypothesis that the average time of all operators is equal at a 5% level of significance. (Given $F_{0.05\,,(2,9)}$ =4.26) **10**

Bachelor Of Computer Application
(Bca - Revised)
Chapter 18: Term Examination, December 2022
Bcs-040: Statistical Techniques

Time: 2 Hours
Maximum Marks: 50
Note:

Attempt both sections, i.e., Section A and Section B.
Attempt any four questions from Section A.
Attempt any three questions from Section B.
Use of non-scientific calculator is allowed.

Section A

1. In a study on the per capita income for a particular year in a city, the following weekly observations were made:

Per Capita Income (₹) (1 k = 1000)	Number of Weeks
14k–15k	5
15k–16k	10
16k–17k	20
17k–18k	9
18k–19k	6
19k–20k	2

Draw a histogram and frequency polygon on the same scale. **5**

2. A problem of statistical techniques is given to three students A, B, and C whose chances of solving it are 1/2, 1/3 and 1/4 , respectively.
(i) What is the probability that the problem will be solved?
(ii) What is the probability that only one of them will solve the problem correctly? **5**

3. Determine the mean and median for the following data: **5**

Marks	No. of Students
0–10	10
10–20	9
20–30	25
30–40	30
40–50	16
50–60	10

4. Box A contains 5 red and 4 blue balls. Box B contains 2 red and 5 blue balls. A ball is drawn at random from each box. Find the probability that one is red and the other is blue. **5**

5. A statistics professor has given four tests. A student scored 75, 65, 80, and 95, respectively, in the four tests. The professor decides to determine his grade by randomly selecting a sample of 2 test scores. Construct the sampling distribution for this process. **5**

Section B

6. Find and plot the regression line of y on x for the data given below: **10**

Speed (km/hr)	Stopping distance (in feet)
30	160
40	240
50	330
60	435

7. In a partially destroyed laboratory, the legible record of analysis of correlation of data is as follows: Variance of x=9, Regression equations: **10**

(i) $8x-10y+66=0$

(ii) $4x-18y-214=0$

What were:

(a) The means of x and y,

(b) The coefficient of correlation between xand y, and

(c) The standard deviation of y?

8. (a) Compare simple random sampling with replacement and simple random sampling without replacement. **2**

(b) Define time series and discuss various components of a time series. **4**

(c) Write short notes on the following: **2+2**

(i) t-test

(ii) Properties of a good estimator

9. The table given below shows the relation between the performance of students in Statistics and Computer Science. Test the hypothesis that the performance in Statistics is independent of the performance in Computer Science using a 5% level of significance. (Given that $\chi^2_{(0.05,4)}=9.49$) **10**

	Computer Science		
	High Grade	**Medium Grade**	**Low Grade**
Statistics			
High Grade	36	72	42
Medium Grade	34	122	44
Low Grade	50	56	44

Bachelor Of Computer Application
(Bca - Revised)
Chapter 19: Term Examination, June 2023
Bcs-040: Statistical Techniques

Time: 2 Hours
Maximum Marks: 50
Note:

Attempt both sections, i.e., Section A and Section B.
Attempt any four questions from Section A.
Attempt any three questions from Section B.
Use of non-scientific calculator is allowed.

Section A

1. The following data shows the marks obtained by 100 students in a statistics examination. Construct a histogram and find the mode graphically. **5**

Marks	No. of Students
10–20	8
20–30	12
30–40	20
40–50	30
50–60	18
60–70	12

2. Calculate the mean, median, and standard deviation from the following data: **5**

Wages (in ₹)	No. of Workers
500–600	5
600–700	10
700–800	15
800–900	20
900–1000	25

3. A bag contains 5 red balls and 3 black balls. Two balls are drawn at random without replacement. Find the probability that: **5**
(i) Both balls are red.
(ii) One ball is red and the other is black.
(iii) None of the balls drawn are red.

4. A die is rolled 360 times, and the following frequencies are obtained: **5**

Face of Die	1	2	3	4	5	6
Frequency	60	50	40	70	90	50

Test whether the die is unbiased at a 5% level of significance. (Given $\chi^2_{0.05}(5)=11.07$)

5. Two candidates contested an election. Candidate A received 65% of the total votes cast. If 100 votes are chosen at random, find the probability that exactly 70 votes are for candidate A. **5**

Section B

6. Fit a straight line to the following data using the method of least squares: **10**

X	1	2	3	4	5
y	2	5	7	10	12

Estimate y for x=6.

7. Perform an analysis of variance (ANOVA) on the following data to determine if the treatment effect is significant at the 5% level of significance: (Given $F_{(2,12)}$ (0.05)=3.88) **10**

Treatment	A	B	C
Yield	15	18	21
	20	22	25
	22	20	24

8. A company manufactures car tires. The life of a tire follows a normal distribution with a mean of 40,000 km and a standard deviation of 3,000 km. Find the probability that a tire will last:
(i) More than 42,000 km
(ii) Between 38,000 km and 42,000 km
(Given Z=0.8413for 1 standard deviation) **10**

9. Explain stratified random sampling. A population of 1000 people is divided into 3 strata. If the sizes of the strata are 400, 300, and 300 respectively, and a sample of 100 is to be selected, determine the sample size from each stratum using proportional allocation. **10**

Bachelor Of Computer Application
(Bca - Revised)
Chapter 20: Term Examination, December 2023
Bcs-040: Statistical Techniques

Time: 2 Hours
Maximum Marks: 50
Note:

Attempt both sections, i.e., Section A and Section B.
Attempt any four questions from Section A.
Attempt any three questions from Section B.
Use of non-scientific calculator is allowed.

Section A

1. (a) An electric bulb manufacturing company chooses a random sample of 10 bulbs, received from one of the suppliers. It determines the life of each bulb. The results (in thousands of hours) are as follows:

3, 4.5, 5.0, 4.2, 4.8, 4.2, 5.1, 4.0, 4.2, 4.5

Compute and analyze a point estimate of the mean life of the bulbs received from the supplier. **3**

(b) Compare parametric and non-parametric tests. **2**

2. An insurance company has insured 1000 truck drivers, 3000 car drivers, and 6000 scooter drivers. The probabilities that the truck, car, and scooter drivers meet with an accident are 0.2, 0.04, and 0.25, respectively. One of the insured persons meets with an accident. What is the probability that the person is a car driver? **5**

3. A football manufacturing company wants to check the variation in the weight of balls. For this, 25 samples (each of size 4) are selected. The weight of each ball is measured (in grams), and the sum of sample averages and sum of sample ranges were found to be:

$\sum_{i=1}^{25} \bar{x}_i = 4010\ grams\ and\ \sum_{i=1}^{25} R_i = 72\ grams$ Compute the control limits for the $\bar{X}$ and R charts. Given: A_2=0.729, D_3=0, and D_4=2.282. **5**

4. The frequency distribution of the accidental data of the factory for the last 50 weeks is shown below:

No. of Accidents	No. of Weeks
0–5	8
5–10	22
10–15	10
15–20	8
20–25	2

Draw the histogram and calculate the average number of accidents per week. **5**

5. In order to test whether there is any significant difference between the proportion of safety consciousness of men and women while driving a car, a study was conducted. The study includes a sample of 300 men and 300 women. Out of 300 men, 130 said that they used seat belts, and out of 300 women, 90 said that they used seat belts. Based on the given data, test the claim that there is no significant difference between the proportion of safety consciousness of men and women while driving a car at a 5% level of significance. (Given $Z_{0.025}$=1.96) **5**

6. A company manufactures two types of machines (A and B). The manager of the company tests a random sample of 50 machines of Type A and 60 machines of Type B and found the following information:

Type	Mean Life (hours)	Standard Deviation (hours)
Type A	1300	50
Type B	1200	60

Obtain the 99% confidence interval for the difference in the average life of the two types of machines. (Given $Z_{0.005}$= 2.58) **5**

Section B

7. To enforce the speed limit at four different locations in the city, the Police plans to install radar traps at each of the locations L1, L2, L3, and L4. The radar traps at each location are operated 40%, 30%, 20%, and 30% of the time, respectively. If a person who is speeding on his way to work has probabilities of 0.2, 0.1, 0.5, and 0.2, respectively, of passing through these locations, what is the probability that he will receive a speeding ticket? Find also the probability that he will receive a speeding ticket at locations L1, L2, L3, and L4. **10**

8. Find and plot the regression line of yyy on xxx, for the data given below: **10**

Speed (km/hr)	30	40	50	60
Stopping Distance (ft)	160	240	330	435

9. A chemical firm wants to determine how four catalysts differ in yield. The firm runs the experiment in three of its plants, namely A, B, and C. In each plant, the yield is measured with each catalyst. The yield (in quintals) is as follows:

Catalyst	1	2	3	4
Plant A	2	1	2	4
Plant B	3	2	1	3
Plant C	1	3	3	1

Perform an ANOVA and comment on whether the yield due to a particular catalyst is significant or not at a 5% level of significance. (Given $F_{3,6}$= 4.76) **10**

10. In order to study the impact of air pollution on households, a random sample of 200 households was selected from each of the two communities. The respondents in each house were asked whether or not anyone in the house was bothered by air pollution. The responses are tabulated below (Given $\chi^2_{1(0.05)}$=3.841 α=0.05):

Community	Yes	No	Total
I	43	157	200
II	81	119	200
Total	124	276	400

Can the researcher conclude that the two communities are bothered differently by air pollution? **10**